I Really Need You to Hear This

I Really Need You to Hear This

Kim Bearden
Illustrated by Madison Hunt

I Really Need You to Hear This
© 2025 Kim Bearden and Madison Hunt

All rights reserved. No part of this publication may be reproduced in any form or by any electronic or mechanical means, including information storage and retrieval systems, without permission in writing by the publisher, except by a reviewer who may quote brief passages in a review. For information regarding permission, contact the publisher at books@daveburgessconsulting.com.

> This book is available at special discounts when purchased in quantity for educational purposes or for use as premiums, promotions, or fundraisers. For inquiries and details, contact the publisher at books@daveburgessconsulting.com.

Published by Dave Burgess Consulting, Inc.
Vancouver, WA
DaveBurgessConsulting.com

Library of Congress Control Number: 2025937381
Paperback ISBN: 978-1-956306-95-8
Ebook ISBN: 978-1-956306-96-5

Cover and interior design by Liz Schreiter
Cover and interior illustrations by Madison Hunt
Edited and produced by Reading List Editorial
ReadingListEditorial.com

*To all my students, past and present.
You have taught me how to listen with
my heart and my eyes.*

*And to Nancy Quattlebaum, the best teacher
I ever had. Your life was too short, but you
left an indelible mark upon this world.
Thank you for truly seeing me.*

Contents

Prelude 1
Invisible 3
Lunch 6
Grief 9
Sometimes I Take Things out on You 12
I'd Rather Take the Bus 14
Drama 17
Grownup Stress 19
Small 21
Big 23
Proud 25
Perfection 27
Checked Out 30
Behind the Door 32
Targeted 34
Grades 37
A Joke 40
Hovering 42
Walls 44
ADHD 46
I Listen with My Eyes 50
Compared 52
There Is Nothing I Do Well 54
Present 56
The Sidelines 58
Broken Promises 60
Afraid 63
Listen 65

Sorry	67
Bully	69
Chasing the Wind	71
Weight	74
Say No	76
Empty	78
Taking Sides	80
Too Late	82
The Cycle	84
Pillow Talk	86
I'm Going through Stuff	88
Energy	90
Labeled	92
I Lied	94
Crush	96
Outside the Circle	98
Daddy	100
If I Were Claire	102
If I Were Sam	104
Leadership	105
The Unraveling	107
Overscheduled	109
I Learn Differently	112
Loud	114
Puberty	116
A Good Day	118
It's Hard to Be Young	120
Discussion Questions	124
About Kim Bearden	126
About Madison Hunt	128
More from Dave Burgess Consulting, Inc.	129

Prelude

I really need you to hear the thoughts
Of those whose voices are often not
Amplified as they should be
Sometimes the words are hard, you see

And if you do not listen well
Then they will choose no more to tell
You how it feels to be in their place
What it's like to be in a space

Where no one seems to really get
The struggles you face, the pain, and yet
We tell young people they'll be okay
But what if they're not? We must stay

Aware, alert, and vigilant so
No matter what, they'll always know
That we'll remain and not abandon
We will tell truths and not give random

Words to comfort them in vain
But words that heal and help maintain
A relationship that's built on trust
If you are willing, then you must

Absorb these poems with open heart
Let every word ignite a spark
I wrote these lines, but their pain is true
And now, dear reader, it's up to you

Invisible

Third row over, fifth seat back
I am the one sitting still near the stack
Of books on your shelf, and papers piled high
Yes, I am quiet, but I am not shy

You put me here knowing I will be good
You sit kids near me so they'll act like they should
I do all my homework and ace every test
On every essay, I've become the best

And although I work hard, I must confess
I keep to myself and rarely express
My thoughts and ideas, although I'm so smart
It's hard to care much, to give things much heart

When you are invisible, it seems much more sensible
To be here and be clear that I am not part
Of meaningful moments—I just exist
My name just remains on the student class list

Third row over, fifth seat back
I should take this class time to rest and relax
You don't call on me or ask me to speak
I could volunteer, but it's not what I need

To do 'cause invisible's working for me
And the value I add is not something you see
I've finally checked out—not that you care
I'll still get good grades if I chill in my chair

I don't think that you think about what I am thinking
In fact, when you look at me, I see you blinking
Sometimes it seems that you might have a question
But the more we've gone round and round in our
class sessions
I've figured it out. It is a shame
I now know the rules to this pointless end game
You don't ask because, well . . . you don't know my name

Invisible

Lunch

The lunchroom buzz drifts down the halls
Through the doors into the stalls
I'm hiding here 'til lunchtime's done
Because there's not a single one
Of you who lets me sit with you
So what am I supposed to do?

It happens every single day
I'm standing here with my lunch tray
There's so much that I want to say
But you simply look away
You move your purse into the chair
You pile your papers and backpack there

Lunch

Making it clear that I'm not part
Of your clique, and if I start
To place my tray and join your space
You'll roll your eyes and make a face
You'll find a way to make me leave
And so I pause, afraid to breathe

I feel so awkward and aware
That everybody sees me there
My cheeks burn hot—can't halt, can't stop
My trembling tears, and there's not
A single classmate there who cares
Enough to spare a single chair

I know I don't have the best clothes
You look at me—turn up your nose
Sometimes I try to talk too much
But it's because there is such
A hunger for a single friend
Or at least somewhere I can spend
Thirty minutes every day
Instead of running to this place

Retreating, disappearing, crying, fearing
Anxiety rises, and I'm peering
Through a crack in the stall door
It smells—there's urine on the floor
My stomach aches—I need some food

But there's nothing else to do
I know this makes me weirder, yet
I know I never will forget
That when I was a kid in school
No one liked me . . . including you

Grief

The empty chair at the end of the table
Forever reminds me that I am not able
To talk to you ever again
You are gone forever, and
The emptiness drowns me—it wraps around me
No space for solace, piercing pain surrounds me

Battered and broken—it pulls me under
I cannot sleep because I wonder
How to live when you do not
How to breathe when you cannot
There is no way to understand
How you'll never hold my hand

You'll never comfort me again
How do I begin where your life ends?
You promised that you'd fight to stay
You did your best until the day
When darkness devoured me—left me broken
Too many words were left unspoken

And now I struggle to utter a sound
I weep and wrap my arms around
Myself to keep my shoulders from shaking
How do I cease continuous aching?

The silence screams loudly in this stark space
Where fond family memories used to be made

Now every room and each empty chair
Is a ruthless reminder that you are not there
Can you hear me? Can you see me?
Can you please replace and be me?
I'm sinking in shadows, deeper still
God grant me some grace in some way—fill

This sorrow inside and help me to heal
I pray for peace and hope I'll feel
Whole again and remember days bright
Before you were sick and forced with that fight
But though you have left, you are not gone from me
I'll cling to your memory in all that I see

For now, I'll step slowly, but still I'll push through
I'm certain that it's what you'd want me to do
I'm told as time passes, I'll start to stand stronger
Focus on fond things and good things for longer
The moments of memories were mere seconds with you
But I'll learn be thankful, despite how they flew

Grief

Sometimes I Take Things out on You

Sometimes I take things out on you
I know it's not what I should do
But I'm filled with so much angst
Sometimes it feels I'm up against

The whole wide world and everyone
But I share this with no one
And I know that it's confusing
When other adults say I am choosing

To always be polite and sweet
To every person that I meet
I'm happy! Awesome! Respectful! Kind!
They just don't know how well I hide

The pain I push away and smile
I'm their favorite kid and while
I act the way you raised me to
Why don't I act that way with you?

I know it's not right and it is not fair
That you get the brunt of all my despair

Sometimes I Take Things out on You

One day I'll do better at how I express this
But the true reason I do this, I guess, is

You're always there for me; you never leave
You are more patient than you have to be
You provide comfort; you are my safe space
Although I try hard to push you away

One day I'll know just how to explain
The reasons I say things I know cause you pain
But please believe that despite what I do
I'm grateful you love me, and I still love you

I'd Rather Take the Bus

I think I'd rather take the bus
Than have to listen to you fuss
Did I do my homework? Yes
Did I pass the test? I guess

When is my next history quiz?
This is the way it always is
I know the drive's not very far
But I'm kept captive in the car

And all this negativity
Causes me anxiety
I know the things that should be done
But I just want to scream and run
Can we just play the quiet game?
Your tone is driving me insane

I'd Rather Take the Bus

I'd really rather take the bus
I know I need to earn your trust
But on the way to school is not
The time to remind me I am not
Doing well—I should do more
But didn't you say this the night before?

Nothing changed while I was sleeping
And in the morning, what I am needing
Are positive thoughts to start the day
That might help me make a change

I have to walk into a place
Filled with pressures, stress—a space
Where I'm reminded what I lack
I need for you to have my back

I'd really rather take the bus
If you want us to discuss
How much stuff I need to do
Conversations should take two

I know that your friends' children are
Succeeding more than I by far
I need new friends, my room's not clean,
I need to practice to make the team

I really miss our time together
When we'd laugh and smile whether
Or not I was perfect then
I need to know that parent again

I understand I must do better
I'm working hard to pull it together
And I am studying every night
Doing it right, and despite
I have a ways I need to go
Your nagging's not the way I grow

The bus is slow, dirty, and loud
From all the students acting out
But at least the ceaseless screams
And endless yelling is not at me

Drama

If they gave out an award
For the way you acted toward
Everyone you see at school
Miss Girl Drama would be you

Everyone's your favorite friend
That is, of course, until it ends
When someone else has more appeal
Then your motives are revealed

We tell you secrets that you share
You spread your lies without a care
For how it hurts and causes pain
And yet there's no remorse or shame

You giggle and gossip and toss your hair
While others surround you and worship you there
It's your superpower—they coddle and cower
Yet speak of you like you're a sweet, fragile flower

You're poised and the prettiest—there is no doubt
You buy the best styles as soon as they're out
But your minions are clueless, unable to follow
How under the glitz, your soul is quite hollow

You'll cast a cruel joke at someone's expense
Despite how it cuts them, you will defend
The way you belittle, humiliate
So I cannot affiliate

Myself with you, no matter the cost
And if my popularity's lost
I'd rather be an outcast than
Someone harmful, hurtful, and
Manipulative and just plain mean
When it comes to girl drama, you are the queen

Grownup Stress

My mom is doing the best that she can
She working two jobs, she's tired and
Although she cannot be home with us all
Every night she makes sure that she calls

To check and make sure that I feed
My brothers and sisters and care for their needs
I know that my homework has not yet been done
But my brother was crying because there were none

Of his clothes that were clean 'cause our washing machine
Is broken again and the stains can been seen
And my sister was hungry and wanted to eat
I told her again that potatoes are treats

I had to make sure that both were asleep
Before I could look at the book work for me
I'm fully aware that my grades have been dropping
I'm tired, too, and it should not be shocking

That being a kid with grownup stress
Will obviously keep me from doing my best
Yes, I care, so please do not seethe at me
I need your patience—I do what I must for me

My mom is a good mom, and she's really trying
She just needs some help—there's no denying
That all of this pressure pains me a lot
But my mom and siblings are all that I've got

Because we are struggling for ways to pay rent
This pattern on repeat will defeat us again
So please help me somehow while I'm here at school
I'm hoping for patience and guidance from you

Small

When you are smaller than all of the rest
It can be hard to feel you're the best
At sports, of course, but other things, too
Things that you might not notice so soon
For one thing, my brain works like others my age
Even if my body's not at the right stage
Don't use baby talk and say I am cute
It's really the worst thing that you can do
Don't pick me up—my legs work just fine
Don't ask me to sit on your lap and whine
That you wish that your kids would stay just as small
It doesn't make me feel good at all

When you are smaller than all the rest,
Having a crush can be such a mess
Please don't grin as you say, "Oh, how sweet!"
Do not embarrass me, tease me, or be
Different to me than you would other kids
Treat me just the same—if you did
Then others won't think that somehow I'm damaged
Just because I am vertically challenged
I've heard all the jokes about riding the rides
Using kids' menus and highchairs—besides
Why would you think that's okay to do
Just because I am smaller than you?

Here's the thing: one day I will grow
Into an adult—one who will know
Just who he is and how to be kind
How to see others for more than their size
When I look at people, I'll see deep inside
I'll know who they are by what's in their eyes
But for now, I ask you to give me respect
Know I am more than my height—don't forget
I can still be better than best
Even if I'm smaller than all of the rest

Big

When you are bigger than all of the rest
Others assume that you'll be the best
At sports, of course, but other things too
You're treated much older and more mature, too
For one thing, my brain works like others my age
Even if my body's not at the right stage
Don't say how great it must be to be tall
I should be a model! Play basketball!
Don't talk about how much food I must eat

Or how hard it is to find shoes for my feet
I don't want to hear how you wish you were tall
It doesn't help me or feel good at all

When you are bigger than all the rest
You're expected to be wiser despite all the stress
Don't talk about how I look in my chair
It's embarrassing enough—I'm fully aware
That I tower above other kids; I'm full grown
I'll forever be placed in the photo's back row
It's hard enough for me to fit in
Without pointing out the adult clothes I'm in
I've heard all the jokes about being a giant
Bodyguard, protector, strong, self-reliant
Why would you think that's okay to do
Just because I am bigger than you?

Here's the thing: one day I'll stop growing
I will be an adult—one with a knowing
Of just who he is and how to be kind
How to see others for more than their size
When I look at people, I'll see within
I won't judge who they are by the frame they are in
But for now, I ask you to grant me some grace
My brain is still growing, despite how much space
My body takes up; I am still young inside
Wait 'til my body is matched by my mind

Proud

Today you told me that I made you proud
And when you said those words out loud
I realized how the best things come
When you work hard and earn each one
All the late nights I was struggling
Studying hard while also juggling
All my tasks while others relaxed
And solving problems, completing stacks
Of papers, writing, reading, finding
At my desk with you reminding
Me it would be worth the pain
It was the truth—I'm not the same
I am smarter, I stand taller
I'm a leader, not a follower
I am capable—I have worth
This has inspired a new thirst
To live with excellence—do my best
To set examples for the rest

Today you said I made you proud
I saw your eyes and realized how
They twinkled, sprinkled with delight
It let me know that I ignite
Happiness inside of you

And I also felt it, too
Thank you—you kept pushing me
On this new trajectory
You didn't yell or scream or fuss
You just showed up—said I must
Do my best. That's all you asked
You helped me when there was a task
Where I needed your support
But you made me do the work
I get it now. I understand
You tug while letting go of my hand
What a difference you have made
I know now I've got what it takes

Perfection

Whenever I study my own reflection
I find frequent flaws, and I want perfection
My nose isn't straight; I wrestle with weight
Spots freckle my skin; my posture's not great
My smile should be wider; my teeth should be brighter
And the gap makes me grin like a battered prize fighter

My eyelashes lack luster; my dull eyes a drab color
And my haggard, thin hair should be anything other
Than the drab, dull mop that's atop of my head
It's tangled and mangled like I've been in bed
But instead I attempted to tame it for hours
I even conditioned it twice in the shower

I desperately desire a new manicure
But even with all that help, I'm sure
My nails will never look like hers—
Elongated, elegant, painted with swirls
My freakish feet are as rough as raw leather
My toes—curved and crooked—I wish they looked better

My voice is vexing; I hobble like a horse
And if you witnessed me dance, of course
You'd know that my thighs are tubby and chubby

My stomach is squishy—I know 'cause I study
Myself every time that I take all of those selfies
I see then what's wrong and just what I should be

I scroll without stopping—peruse the perfection
How could I not help but reel from rejection
I'm convinced what is beautiful and see the selection
Of those who are flawless—they get more affection
Perhaps if I filter myself, those online
Will see *me* as perfect and they'll think that I'm

The one to be envied, copied, admired
They will be influenced, and they'll be inspired
To learn that they're less than . . . because of me
And my posted pictures—then maybe I'll see
That perfection's an illusion . . . I'll be relieved
To realize it's all fake . . . it's all make believe

Perfection

Checked Out

Our teacher doesn't like her job—we know without a doubt
It's crystal clear, and we fear she truly has checked out
She doesn't react when kids are acting up and don't behave
She used to try to keep class calm, but now she always caves

Her lessons are not planned at all—we do page after page
Of worksheets in tired textbooks that are older than our age
We know we shouldn't ask for help, though help is what we need
Instead we learn from what we see while scrolling on our feed

She never gets up from her desk—she slumps while sitting there
The minutes move like hours, and it's more than we can bear
We know she doesn't notice us—she has hollow eyes
No matter what we do in class, she doesn't seem surprised

When she speaks, she says she's tired from all she has to do
She complains of aches and pains—each day there's something new
I get confused on how to use all of this wasted time
If we do not learn this stuff, won't we be behind?

Checked Out

I'm sad for her—I really am—I know that something's up
But I'm also sad for us—we need to know this stuff
Our teacher doesn't like her job—we know without a doubt
But for our sake, she must leave this place unless you help her out

Behind the Door

At the door I hesitate before I turn the key
What sorrow scene or trauma theme will be inside for me?
I have two moms with the same name, but no two days are just the same
Sometimes she smiles, but when she drinks, she says that I'm to blame
I have a dad who stays one way, but he is always mad
So I must shift and silently sit to convince him I'm not bad

I learned in school 'bout coping tools to keep my mind intact
But how the heck do I protect my heart and deal with that?
My heart beats fast—it always lasts until I turn the knob
Every day I feel this way—my happiness is robbed
I hold the words designed to hurt and push them to my gut
And though they're just what they deserve, I'm the one they cut

How is this right that I can't fight to rip this world apart?
There's no reprise for all their lies, and I need a new start
I want to run away today and get so far away today
But I know of nowhere else to go, and so I've got to stay
At the door I hesitate before I turn the key
If you could know how far I'd go if only I could leave

Behind the Door

Targeted

When you always think that it's always me
I wonder if your eyes can see
I'm not the one who threw the book
I didn't say that or give him that look
But somehow it's my name that you call
Even when I did nothing at all
I've not been perfect, but I've been pretty good
Even when others don't do what they should
Yes, I have done some dumb things before
I was going through something, so please don't keep score

When you always think that it's always me
Deep inside, it baffles me
I try not to argue or roll my eyes
I try to keep calm 'cause I'm not surprised
But jeez! I'm so tired of you taking aim
Day after day, I am always to blame
Perhaps if you set aside some of your bias
You would find that some who seem perfect and pious
Can be quite devious—acting mischievously
Despite what you heard from their old teachers previously

Targeted

When you always think that it's always me
I guess I'm the target that you think you need
I'll just take the fall 'cause my class down the hall
Is different from yours, and she sees it all
She's consistent, firm, and never neglectful
She holds her high standards, and all are respectful
She laughs a lot, but she won't accept
Misbehavior, foolishness, or anything less
Than excellence. She's genuine, and she doesn't fake this
I believe in myself because she sees my greatness

When you always think that it's always me
It's funny that your eyes can't see
Me the way that teacher does
Perhaps if you did, it would change things because
Kids will be kids, but we all need someone
Who forgets past mistakes and believes we'll become
Adults with great purpose—I'll still succeed
She sees that. She knows that it's not always me

Grades

Whenever I get a grade of B,
It's a colossal catastrophe
My heartbeat stops and skips a beat,
And I choke; I cannot breathe

My hands start shaking, my forehead sweats,
And I simply can't forget
About my fears that release my tears;
I'm filled with remorse and regret

I swiftly spiral to a place
Where my thoughts are rushed and raced
I ponder if I'll pass the class.
Will I forever be erased?

When my whole identity
Is being smart, what will I be
If I'm not best of all the rest?
There's nothing left for me

My family will be so ashamed
They'll criticize, no longer claim
Me when I'm not still on the top
They'll disown me, change my name

Grades

I won't succeed in life—indeed,
I won't get the job I need
I won't have friends who will defend
And help me when I plead

No one will love me anymore;
If I knock they'll shut the door
I'll be a stranger who lives in great danger
I'll never be much more

And I bet my dear old pets
Will walk away and hate me, yet
I won't have funds to find where they run
Because I'll be in debt

So it is clear why I must adhere
To making an A on this test right here
I cannot abandon these thoughts that are random
Anytime failure's near

I am so tired, but it's how I'm wired;
I am overwhelmed with my misery
But I will work more just to ensure
That I never again make a B

A Joke

The time you made fun of me in that cruel way
I don't know if you knew how your words would stay
They'd forever remain—I would not be the same
They changed how I'd see myself; I have reframed

The person I thought I was; I'm now just a joke
I repeatedly replay the words that you spoke
And perhaps even worse is the way that you planned
A scheme to demean me and humiliate me and

You secretly told them the scheme of your plot
To pretend that you liked me when, in fact, you did not
I stood still with a smile, not seeing all the while
That the joke was on me and your actions were vile

I wish I was able to move on and let go
But it belittled and broke me, and I want you to know
The sting of the thing that you did to me still
Cuts 'cause I'm certain it gave you a thrill

To see how the others all joined in and jeered
I looked like a loser in front of my peers
I cannot believe that I thought I could see
Something that made you seem special to me

A Joke

Hovering

When you hover over me
You steal my space and I can't breathe
The way you're always watching, waiting
It can be so suffocating

    I wonder why you cannot trust
    That I will do what things I must
    I follow and obey your rules every day
    I listen and do everything that you say

        But when you are constantly watching me
        It raises my anxiety
        I can't stumble or mix things up
        Because if I do, you'll pick me up

If you keep on covering me
Responsible I'll never be
I need to know it's okay to fail
To miss the mark of small details

Hovering

You do not acknowledge I'm growing up
And if you're always showing up
To point out ways I'm weak, not wise
You should not become surprised

                      If I never take the lead
                      Accomplish big goals to succeed
                      I'll be scared to use my voice
                      I'll second-guess and doubt each choice

Because if you don't think I am able
I'll start to believe you and you'll enable
Me to be less than—I'll be dependent—
An adult who never finds my independence

    I love that you're there for me and that you care for me
        You do everything—you are everywhere for me
           I like when you help—that is just mothering
           But I'll never grow with this continuous hovering

Walls

When I weld my walls of steel
It helps me hide the way I feel
Not just from you, but from myself
I've tucked it all upon a shelf
As a way to survive, I've
Opted not to feel alive, I've
Chosen numbness over pain
And in this state I can remain
Safe and not feel all the sorrow
It will still be here tomorrow
But I guess that the worst part is
I've forgotten where my heart is
When you wall out all that aches
Joy does not refill the space
When you cover up despair,
Healing does not happen there

I want to live, not just exist
But the hardest part of this
Is trusting when the walls come down
That you will always stick around
I know it can be hard to stay
When I've pushed you far away
However badly I've behaved

Walls

I really hope you'll find a way
To be a gate, to build a bridge
Remind me how to choose to live
Help me learn again to trust
If you do, I'll know I must
Begin to chip these walls of steel
And live again . . . this time for real

ADHD

When you pay attention to everything
You hear every voice and every text ping
Pencils tapping, gum unwrapping, binders snapping, children laughing
It might seem like it should make you happy
But it can be hard to know just what is happening
If you are not like this, you just cannot know that
You feel overwhelmed, but you cannot show that
Your mind keeps on racing, and you cannot slow that
When you pay attention to everything

When you pay attention to everything
You sometimes forget what things you should bring
Your items get lost, despite what they cost
Your dirty clothes sometimes get mixed with the washed
You misplace your phone, and you lose your shoes
You can't find your homework right when it is due
And despite the fact that you try your hardest
Your stuff is a mess, and the worst part is
You don't want to do this; it's not where your heart is
When you pay attention to everything

ADHD

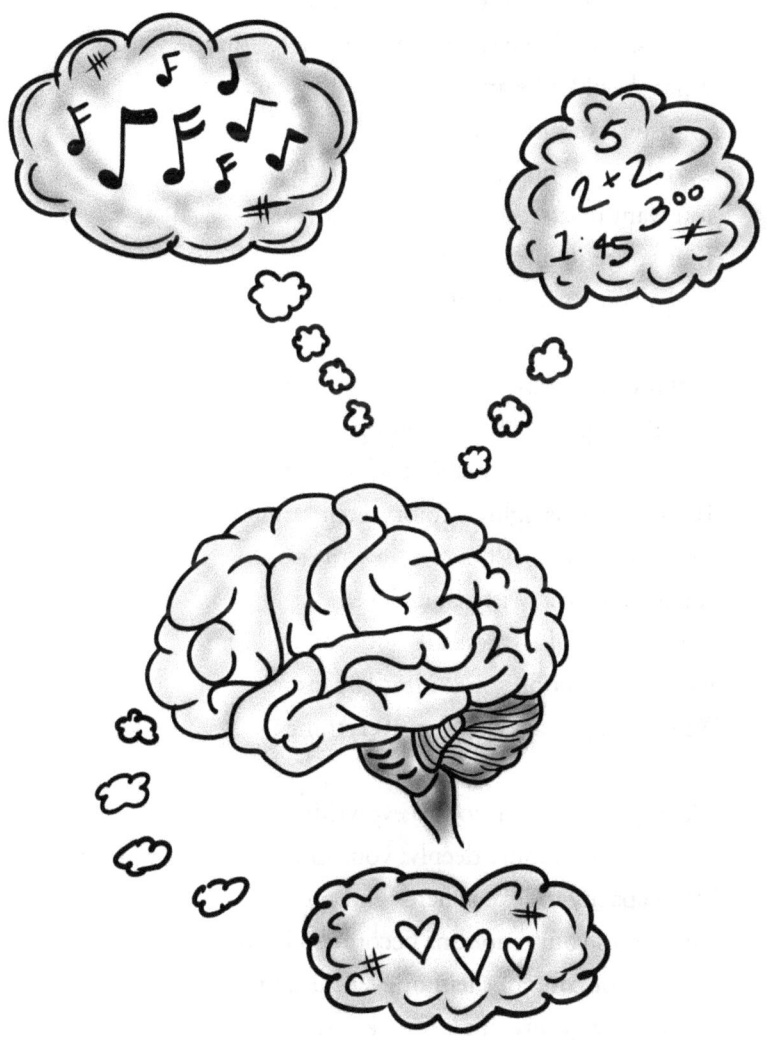

When you pay attention to everything
Time slips away until alarms ring
There is so much to do, but sometimes you freeze
The task should be simple, but you're lost in the weeds
What should take an hour sometimes takes weeks
So instead of just doing it, you just want to leave
It stresses you out, and others can't see
You want to do it—they don't believe
That you're doing your best, despite what it seems
When you pay attention to everything

When you pay attention to everything
You often spend time imagining
You are able to dream about what things could be
The sunshine is lighter, colors seem brighter
You're often an artist, a poet, a writer
You are creative, witty, and clever
Boring and dull—these are not ever
Words to describe you—ideas last forever
When you pay attention to everything

When you pay attention to everything
You feel things more deeply; your moods sometimes swing
Your capacity to love is fierce and intense
Sometimes your emotions become so immense
You cannot contain them or even sustain them
Others often don't think it makes sense
But your heart is full and ready to share
Even when hurting, you can't help but care

ADHD

You just wish that others could be more aware
That your joy is real and so is your pain
Remaining calm can be hard to contain
But it's what makes you special and not just the same
As those who retreat and just stay in one lane
Although you are often misunderstood
You should not change yourself even if you could because
You are magnificent—life is good
When you pay attention to everything

I Listen with My Eyes

It might come as a surprise
That I listen with my eyes
You tell me ways that I can be good
And handle hurt and that I should
Always be honorable, honest, and kind
Perhaps you should know that I ask in my mind
Why your actions don't match all your words
You often do cruel things and actions that hurt
And although you tell me the choices to choose
The choices are not ones followed by you

I know that you say things that sound really wise
But I am still listening to you with my eyes
You are often impatient, mean, and snappy
You choose to do things to make others unhappy
You are selfish and seem to want all the attention
You make it about you, and should I mention
The world does not always revolve around you
And just because you hurt, we need not hurt too
I want you to know that I really need
An example to follow and take the lead
Someone who knows the impact of her actions
And proves that good character brings satisfaction

I Listen with My Eyes

And no, you should not receive a big prize
When you say all you've done for me, look at my eyes
You don't have to remind me that you put me first
And sacrificed so many things since my birth
Did you really give up all your hopes and your dreams
Because I exist? If so, then it seems
Like your life with me is full of regrets
You tell me you love me, adore me, and yet
You keep reminding me with things that you do
That I am too much, and I burden you

I'll trust you more if you drop this disguise
You words do not fool me—look into my eyes
I love but don't like you; I don't want to be
A parent who acts the way you act with me
You're not a victim; I'm not a villain
You can still fix this, but you must be willing
To stop with this show and be someone real
Listen to others and care how they feel
We'll both be happier the day you realize
That your words and your actions are never aligned

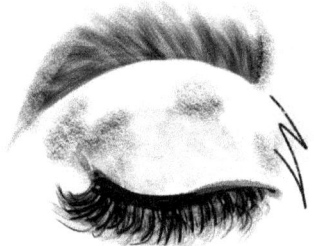

Compared

Yes, she is great, but I'm not my sister
I know she's so smart and don't need you to list her
Accolades and awards—I know what she's won
Wherever I go, I'm told all she has done

Do I look up to her? Yes, how I love her
But stop making me feel like I should be another
Version of me. She leaves you in awe
But the way you relay that implies that I'm flawed

It's hard for me not to leave you disappointed
When she is so perfect, chosen, anointed
I see she is beautiful, popular, poised
I know I embarrass you, make you annoyed

I'm a good person who's figuring things out
But when you compare us, you cause me to doubt
My value, my worth, the way that you love me
For the rest of my life, I'll know she's above me

Do you know how it feels to be constantly measured
By someone you love—imagine the pressure
At school and with friends, but even at home
I'm part of our family, yet feel all alone

Compared

My sister's magnificent, and she deserves
The honors she gets, and I'm happy for her
But just 'cause we're sisters who share a last name
It doesn't mean we're designed just the same

There Is Nothing I Do Well

I know that everyone can tell
That there is nothing I do well
They know I've tried to make the team
No matter what, it always seems
That I'm too small, too weak, too slow
There is too much I don't know

I lack the skill, I'm slack during drills
I cannot aim, shoot, and still
I tried to show that I've got something
But each time I felt like nothing
That I did was good enough
So, I tried some other stuff

I studied hard to win debate
But I wrestle to relate
My thoughts too well when I rush
My palms get sweaty; I panic and blush
So art club seemed like a way to impress
But my paintings were worse than all of the rest

Next, I auditioned for the play
Forgot my lines and ran away
So I tried out for the band
But I can't play an instrument and
I don't even hear the beat
That's why I dance with two left feet

There Is Nothing I Do Well

I cry, I hide, fight fear inside
Please know that I've really tried
I pushed myself to prove I'm strong
But I keep failing and doing things wrong
I hope that when you look at me
You'll notice something I can't see

I long to find I've got a gift
Can you help me look for it?
I need to know that I'm not less
I'm a work in progress, I guess
I hope that someday someone will tell
Me that there's something that I can do well

Present

I am not sure if this somehow makes sense
But more than your presents, I love that you're present
The clothes are chic, the games are great
You give me good gifts—there is no debate
But I hope you know, and I hope it is clear
What matters most is when you are here
You show your support for all that I do
So my favorite gift is the time spent with you

When you tell me stories about way back when
I imagine you like you are young once again
Your smile twinkles, and despite all your wrinkles
We connect like we are the best of old friends
When we take walks and get lost in the blocks
Of the neighborhood simply because of our talks
I feel important, loved, and adored
I see that you see me, and what is more

You lift me, you cheer me in all that I do,
But the greatest of gifts is just being with you
The more that we do this, the better it makes it
To talk when things aren't good and things are at stake, it
Creates a foundation on which we can build
Even when you're mad or I am strong-willed

Present

You show up, you listen, you come to events
Thank you for being a parent who's present

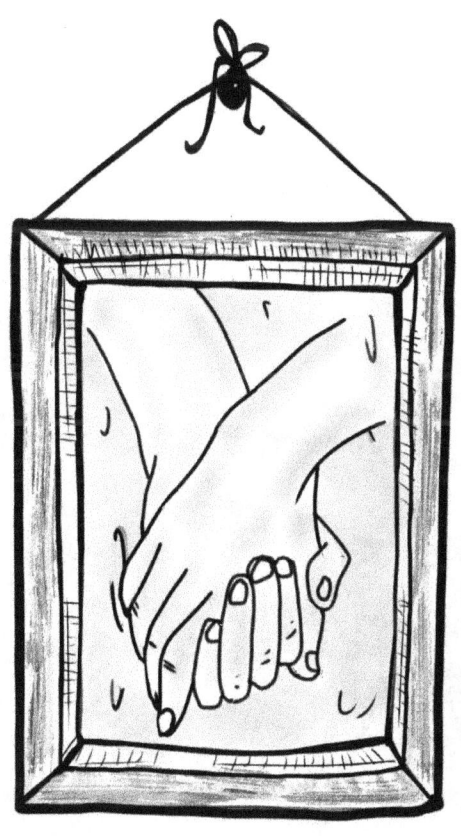

The Sidelines

I know you are my biggest fan
But please don't coach me from the stands
While you're always screaming, yelling
My real coach is also telling
Me what I should do instead
It really messes with my head

The Sidelines

I want to play well, do well, stay well
And when you're shouting every game, well
It makes me feel like I can never
Do what you want, and whoever
I try to please, one will be mad
I have to respect you both, I have
To be my best, but instead now I'm
Playing two ways at the very same time

I know you have big dreams for me
Scholarship goals and teams for me
To do the things you wanted to
But is this about me or you?
You push me hard, and I can take it
But please be careful not to make it
Where I hate the game instead
Of loving it 'cause now I dread
How you behave and embarrass me
Please don't coach; be a parent to me

Broken Promises

When you don't do what you say you will do
I wish you could know what those words put me through
I often spend hours sitting and waiting
Internally hoping, wishing, and praying
Broken promises build up and they keep weighing
Me down—until my heart keeps debating
With my mind about what is the truth
When you don't do what you say you will do

When you don't do what you say you will do
I sometimes wait hours hoping you will come through
I sit on the stairs wondering why you're not there
Making excuses and thinking about where
On earth you could be that's more important than me
It can't always be traffic or work—I can see
That you tell lies—it makes me despise
Myself because I can't help that I cry
I hate that it hurts—I hope to be stronger
But it is harder and harder the longer
I wait for you to become someone who
Does the things that you say you will do

When you don't do what you say you will do
I am embarrassed, and I tell the lies, too
I say you can't make it for reasons I fake that

Broken Promises

Force me to constantly cover for you
I convince other people that you really care
Of course there's a reason that you are not there
And no matter how often I'm asked the questions
I come up with excuses, meetings, and sessions
That you had to go to—you're in demand
But deep inside I feel second-hand
Like items discarded and thrown away
But I keep thinking that maybe one day
You will show up and be someone new
Someone who'll do what they say they will do

Because you don't do what you say you will do
One day I'll have no more patience for you
I'll move on, and you'll be left waiting
Sitting alone and wishing and praying
You'll be old, and you'll feel alone
Perhaps then you'll finally step up and own
Up to your pitiful promises and lies
Perhaps then you'll wish you'd taken the time
To put me first and be who you should be
A parent who proved that you truly loved me
I'll build a family—my kids will never
Wonder why we don't spend our time together
Life is short, and I won't forget
You were responsible for me, and yet
You were too selfish. So shame on you
You never did what you said you would do

Afraid

You ask me to stop always being afraid
But how I wish you could spend just one day
Inside of my head to feel how I worry
It happens to me every time I am hurried

I try to be positive—no gloom and doom
To have happy thoughts so there's not any room
For the scenes to play out—to me they seem real
I sweat and regret every time that I feel

A sense of impending doom or of danger
I cannot forget, and what seems much stranger
Is that my worst fears have not ever come true
But I can't stop wondering 'bout what if they do?

What if I get hurt? What if they laugh?
What if I get lost? What if I don't pass?
Anxiety grows—I can barely breathe
I need to be present—hear, touch, and see

So while I'm learning to combat the fear
Don't laugh at me—to me things seem real
Just reassure me it will be all right
When my mind won't rest, the worry clings tight

Listen

It fuels my frustrations when day after day
No one is hearing a thing that I say
I tell you I'm struggling, and you simply hug me
I need you to pay more attention—it bugs me

When your answer's a smile, it can seem condescending
Indifference to my thoughts creates an impending
Wedge between us, and although you are nice
If you don't know my plight, it does not suffice

I seek your solutions and support to help fix
The fear that I'm facing—please know that it is
Overtaking and making me feel like I'm breaking
I cannot escape it while sleeping or waking

It's not just my words that should make you aware
That something's not right—there is something there
Haven't you noticed I've forgotten my friends?
I isolate myself every time that I can

Since I do not matter, I've stopped applying
Myself in my classes—I'm tired of trying
What was the point of the papers I did
If you didn't notice the answers I'd give?

I Really Need You to Hear This

You say that you care, but I still feel ignored
I won't scream what I mean—it won't help me make more
Of my words any clearer despite what I say
So I'll hold it all in me as I fade away

I've given you signs, and I've spoken my mind
I've even told you that I am not fine
So I beg you to hear what I'm saying to you
Truly listen. It's something I need you to do

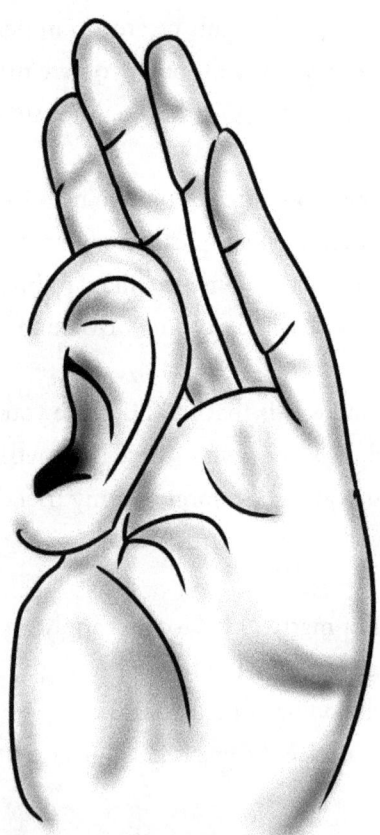

Sorry

The day I did the thing that I did
It left me ill inside, and if
That day on earth I could relive
I hope I would not do the thing that I did

Why did I do it? I'm not sure
Maybe because I can be immature
When I'm insecure, I can become mean
Sometimes I am selfish and want to be seen

I know what I did was reckless and wrong
Maybe I thought it would help me belong
But I'm certain I shouldn't attempt to reduce this
By lingering on a lame list of excuses

Yes, you raised me better than this
It's not your fault, if you think that you miss
What I'm trying to say here; let me make my words clear
Some things—the dumb things—come from weakness and fear

I feel great shame—no one else should be blamed
I'll accept my fate and live up to our name
I will do better and hope that I never
Forget how I hurt you. I'll forever remember

And truly be sorry for the thing that I did
It's not the way that I know I should live
I am hopeful that one day you can forgive
And love me despite that one thing that I did

Bully

I am aware that I'm mean and cruel
Bullying is a potent tool
I force you to follow, to go along
When you are weak, I think I am strong
I use my words—I use my fists
I tell you where you cannot sit
Why do I do it? I pretend that there's power
Whenever I force you to act like a coward
All of the anger I hold on my plate
Spills over, releases itself through my hate
Sometimes it seems I'm cornered and caged
Unable to process my anger, my rage
Deep down inside, I don't feel that I'm safe
I want to run—plot and plan my escape
I hope that no one calls out my bluff
And sees in reality, I'm not so tough

I am aware that I am mean and cruel
I'm feared by the entire school
It helps to squelch the stress on me
When no one else will mess with me
No one knows what's deep inside
If I can keep you terrified
I hate the human who I am

My whole persona is a sham
I want to change, I want to thrive
But I'm just trying to survive, I've
Pushed the guilt and shame away
To deal with on a different day
Until I do, just know it's true
That there is nothing wrong with you
Despite the pain I put you through
The problem's really me, not you

Chasing the Wind

Once upon a time there was
A beautiful little girl
She loved her daddy above all else
He was her entire world

Daddy loved his daughter, too
But he had issues to mend
He tried, but his heart grew restless
And Daddy became Wind

She cried as she chased and begged him to stay
But Wind cannot be tamed
He wanted a life of adventure
She needed him just the same

Sometimes Wind became the Storm
Striking and thundering home
His torrents of anger left her afraid
Broken, unsure, and alone

He always left a path of debris
Sorrow, confusion, despair
But despite the intense pain that he caused
She hated she wished he was there

Wind again, he came less and less
Until she knew him no more
She learned to live without him at all
And forgot the man she adored

The years passed by with Wind out of reach
The scars left behind cut down deep
She grew successful, strong, and quite bold
And claimed there was no one she'd need

Wind also grew older—regretted it all
Mistakes left him broken and scarred
He knew of the pain that he'd caused the girl
And in truth, she still owned his whole heart

Finally ready to see her again
Wind slowed down to Breeze
He asked if they could meet and talk
But in him, she no longer believed

She wanted to see him, she really did—
But she knew he would go back to Wind
She'd learned the ways to protect her own heart
She would never chase him again

Weight

No food is remaining—I've got some explaining
I know you are worried; I know you're complaining
About how my weight, well, it isn't too great
And the body I once liked is now one I hate

The food is a potion that helps sooth emotions
It comforts me when I am going through motions
Of pretending I'm okay when really I'm not
When it comes to my friends, food's the best that I've got

It's always there for me just when I need it
When my heart is hurting, I frequently feed it
A rushing release comes when no words are spoken
But the feeling fleets fast, and then I'm left broken

When I am stressed, I'm sure you have guessed
That eating in excess tricks my mind the best
But after I'm done, I'm filled with such shame
I know it's my fault, and I'm burdened with blame

Why is it so hard to make myself stop?
To learn moderation and know that food's not
A replacement for people . . . it's my addiction
We all need to eat, so the contradiction

Weight

Is how to consume what I need to sustain me
We all have to eat, so can you blame me
For my confusion, my struggle, my pain?
I'm trying my best to simply maintain

A healthy relationship with apple pies,
Potato chips, chocolate chips, crispy french fries
It's horrifically hard, but still I'm annoyed
How I'm tricked into thinking they'll help fill a void

I know you are worried, and you see my fight
I promise to work on it with all my might
Just keep reminding me—you'll always mean
More to me than the food can ever feed

Say No

I know that you choose to go with the flow
But sometimes I wish that you would say no
Yes, you let me do all that I please
Other kids think that they'd love to be me
But I am still young, and I need protection
Sometimes my gut goes in crazy directions
When you won't define needed boundaries for me
I make big mistakes that create misery
I love that you trust me—don't want to complain
It seems weird to ask, but let me explain

Say No

I need some guardrails, not so much freedom
You might not see why, but I know I need them
I want to ensure that I choose the right choice
To do the best thing and still have a voice
So although it is grand that you let me decide
What I should do and when to abide
By the rules of our world, some are not clear
Sometimes my best judgment is blurred by my peers
And sometimes it helps if I have an excuse
Why I can't go or do what they do
So I need your help, and I want you to know
Though sometimes it's hard, please sometimes say no

Empty

Sometimes without warning the emptiness comes
It extends through my limbs, and my body grows numb
The more I keep thinking, the more I start sinking
And sinking—I stare at drawn shades without blinking

I'm stuck in a spiral that's sucking me under
My covers—it's there I'm concealed and you wonder
What you can do or what you did wrong
The answer is nothing . . . nothing's the song

That lingers through darkness inside of my head
It binds me in chains and I'm pinned to my bed
You think I don't care, but really I do
The sorrow inside me is not about you

When I don't respond to your texts or your calls
I do want to answer, it's just it takes all
Of my energy to get through one day at a time
No, nothing happened, but I am not fine

I cannot explain what triggers the void
I just plead for patience when you are annoyed
The shame of it all makes the storm clouds seem stronger
The emptiness builds, and the darkness lasts longer

Empty

After a while, it always subsides
I want to see people and no longer hide
The sun shines again, and I open the door
Returning to life, to you, and what's more

I'll feel once again, but I'm not sure when
The sinking and sinking could start up again
So please don't stop calling, texting, and knocking
Keep coming by and telling me talking
To someone might be a good thing for me
I seek solitude, but it's help that I need

Taking Sides

Please don't tell me the things he did
That ended all you had with him
I'm still your child—it's not my place
To give you space to plead your case

Yes, I love you, and I care
I also love him, and it's not fair
To burden me with what transpired
My taking sides is not required

For what it's worth, he hurt me, too
But what am I supposed to do?
Should we make this all about you?
What about my point of view?
Do I pretend that I don't want a dad?
Live forever hurt and mad?

I know you're in pain; I know you tried
I know he did things that he hides
I know you're the one who chose to stay
He was the one who cheated and played
I know that perhaps I should hate him, too
But it's not something I'm able to do

Taking Sides

All of my feelings are still quite a mess
But it does not mean that I love you less
I hear when you cry behind the door
It breaks my heart, please know for sure
One day when I'm older, I'll be more prepared
To understand things that seem so unfair
But for now, please don't tell me the things that he did
After all, please remember—I'm still just a kid

Too Late

Why do I always shut my door?
Isn't that just what it's for?
Perhaps I need some time alone
To find the comfort you've not shown

When you try but can't relate
It's hard for me to operate
Stop suggesting we are close
You waited too long—it was you who chose

To put yourself and the TV
Before the time you spent with me
We've never been a true family
Even though you pretend to be

You were too busy when I was young
You didn't consider how your distance stung
You never read to me; you still don't eat with me
You have not been the parent that you know that you need to be

So now you've decided you want to connect?
Why should I suddenly give you respect?
I'm not sure I trust you. Why this new change?
If I open up, you'll go back again

Too Late

The pattern always repeats itself
You pick yourself and leave me by myself
You say you need "me time" and it is "self-care"
However, you're clueless and so unaware

That perhaps the reason that you are so lonely
Is because you are selfish and you have ignored me
So excuse me while I go back to my space
My room is my fortress where feelings are safe

The Cycle

Do you really think that I am naive
Enough for me to somehow believe
That this new guy is just a friend?
This is how it always begins

Don't expect me to believe it is different this round
I've fallen for that every time, and I've found
I should not believe when you say he's a friend
It's just the beginning, but I know how this ends

To realize your worth? Don't you deserve more?
There are good men who value and love and adore
Women like you, but instead you're reduced
Diminished, used up, discarded, abused

The anger and sorrow that swirl deep inside
Each time that this happens, it's harder to hide
The dismay I feel and my loss of respect
What made you this way? Why do you neglect

The Cycle

You'll flirt and giggle and dress in less
You'll tell me that he is the very best
Man you've met—he is the one!
And then I'll watch as you become

    A version of you to match his vibe
    While all the while you're dying inside
    You'll laugh at things you don't find funny
    I'll watch when you slip him your hard-earned money

When he raises his voice, I'll see you cower
And it will kill me to watch you relinquish your power
You'll let him move in, his clothes stacked in piles
You'll try to convince me it's just for a while

He'll start taking more and begin disappearing
He'll grow angry with questions, become domineering
Your body will grow weary, your eyes become hollow
You'll tell me you'll fix it as I'm forced to swallow

Pillow Talk

Every time I try to sleep
My pillow tries to talk to me
It tells me I'm not good enough
And makes me replay all the stuff
I said and did and think about
It makes me cringe and then I doubt
Myself and replay it again
I toss and turn and wonder when
I'll fall asleep because it keeps
Laughing, jeering, taunting me

I bunch it up beneath my head
But it still talks, fills me with dread
And if I do not get some sleep
I know how rough my day will be
It says tomorrow I'll be tired
I'm tired now, but I'm still wired
To rewind every single thought
I try to stop, but I cannot
Contemplate how I will doze
Or calmly make my breathing slow

I change positions to my side
But I'm awake despite closed eyes

Pillow Talk

Pillow mocks just to deceive
Me to fear I'll oversleep
Because my body is distressed
I'll miss the alarm if I find rest
I'll nap but I won't slumber well
I wrestle and wiggle and stress until
The sun finally rises; it scoffs again
Pillow smiles. It always wins

I'm Going through Stuff

I know that you know that I'm going through stuff
And being me now can be really rough
But you treat me kindly and not like I'm damaged
Your warmth and your normalcy are how I've managed
To hold it together on difficult days
Your constant support helps in so many ways

You don't ask questions, but I know you'd be there
To shoulder the secrets I'm willing to share
This type of consistency is very new to me—
It's exactly the lift to the weight that's consuming me
At my age, I've seen more than young eyes should bear
But brokenness won't steal my hope for repair

I'm Going through Stuff

I know that you know that I'm going through stuff
Arriving at school on time is kinda tough
You're patient, but you still set high expectations
I see this as an outward manifestation
Of the belief that you've shown that you have in me
I might live in chaos, but it is excellence you see

You know that I'm hurting—my heart sometimes breaks
But you do not define me by others' mistakes
You are the reason that I choose to stay
And truly believe that I'll be okay
I know that you know that I'm going through stuff
But because of you, I still know that I'm enough

Energy

I know my movement makes you tired
But this is how my body's wired
There's energy inside of me
I can't contain—I must release
It out in one of many ways
It's how I learn—it's not just play

When I am in listening mode
It sometimes seems like I'll explode
If I'm stuck to sit without
A break to get this squirming out
You fuss and tell me to be still
You talk and talk and talk until
Anyone—especially me—
Would need to stand
and want to leave
I wish that you
could understand
It stifles me and cuffs
my hands

When I squirm I sense you hate it
But imagine how frustrated
I become when I can't stop

Energy

I want to but I just cannot
I find it challenging to learn
When stillness becomes my concern
Our bodies are designed to move
The parts are there for us to use
I know I need to work on it
But it could help if you could shift
If you'd treat it as a tool
I might not keep distracting you

My other teacher down the hall
Has us stand to answer all
Of the questions—I just mention
That just as one quick suggestion
We use our bodies to make signs
Of the math and graphing lines
We clap our hands and tap our feet
To act out words while in our seat
Arms can even be a tool
To practice punctuation rules
And no—we are not crazy, rowdy—
We're actually calmer when our bodies
Help our brains to learn and grow
We can increase the stuff we know
I'm more alert, focused, relaxed
When I'm in that kind of class
I know my movement makes you tired
But I wish it was required

Labeled

You call us poor, disadvantaged, at-risk
Please help me understand why you insist
On using those labels when you speak of us
Does it make you a savior? Do you think that you must
Categorize us to be able to teach us?
Perhaps if you didn't, you could better reach us

We are scholars, artists, athletes, and writers,
Musicians, scientists, orators, fighters
But what we must fight is often your bias
I need you to realize the talents inside us
Yes, it is true that some struggle and lack
But it's not just the kids who live down near the tracks

There are kids who are wealthy who feel all alone
They don't have the joy that I have in my home
There are some who wear name brands and all the new shoes
But they do not understand math like I do
There are kids with au pairs, mansions, new cars
Who daily feel pain and have holes in their hearts

There are some who have everything one seems to need
But it's not just the things that help children succeed

Labeled

Do their teachers label them? Whisper they're rich?
No-risk? Advantaged? Do they insist
On giving them labels like you give to us?

Those kids—like all kids—need people to teach them
Who challenge, support, and work hard to reach them
Perhaps if you'd consider just calling us scholars
The world would not measure our value by dollars

I Lied

I have a problem deep inside that I'm trying my best
to hide
I know I created it and must bear the weight of it because it
was my own lie
I don't know why I said what I said and made the whole
thing up
But the longer I wait to set the thing straight, the more I'll
lose your trust

At first it was small; I just wanted all of my friends to think
I belonged
But the more it is growing, the more it is showing me that I
was very wrong
The smallest of lies quickly multiply, although I was just
fitting in
But now I've concluded that I'll be excluded because of the
fix I am in

I am not really sure just how I can cure this problem and
make it all right
I'm deeply afraid to tell you I made it all up—I've been
thinking all night
Of ways to undo what I said and just do the honorable
thing and come clean

I Lied

It might be the end of my place with my friends, but at least to me it would mean

That I don't have to be someone other than me; I am fine just to be who I am
If others relish the facts I embellish, they're basing their likes on a scam
One thing that is sure is that I am now cured; I won't make up stories again
It is now clear that my lie came from fear, and I don't need to lie to make friends

Crush

Whenever I see him, I try not to blush
But I'm consumed by this powerful crush
The way that he moves—well, I am not used
To obsessing and stressing so much

Whenever he smiles, my body goes weak
I can't feel a thing from my head to my feet
My words get all jumbled, and I simply mumble
I can't believe he'd choose me

Crush

Does he feel the same way? How do I know?
I wish he would give me a message to show
Me how he feels and if this thing is real
Do things like this go fast or slow?

Do I say that I like him or play hard to get?
If I don't talk to him, he might forget
I even exist—how do I resist?
I fear I'll say words I'll regret

I need to stop wishing that he were mine
Before I met him, I was just fine
This whole thing's exhausting and now it is costing
My sanity—I'm losing my mind

Does loving someone always feel this intense?
If so, I'm not sure that I am convinced
This love thing is worth all the stuff it's unearthed
I do things that do not make sense

So for now, please know I am a little confused
My palms can't stop sweating—I cannot subdue
My heart's constant pounding; it is astounding
That somehow this makes you amused

Outside the Circle

When you're outside the circle and you're not invited
You smile all the while you are hurting inside, and it
Feels like your tears are flaming fires burning
You don't want to care, but you cannot stop yearning

To be included and not feel rejected
But over time, you learn to expect that
You're not a part of their popular group
You don't know their jokes—you're out of the loop

Outside the Circle

You don't understand why you cannot fit in
Why don't they like you? Why can't you be friends?
So you try to be different so you'll be accepted
You change who you are so that you'll feel connected

You do things you wouldn't—you laugh when
you shouldn't
You're socially awkward—you tried but you couldn't
Be an insider without your pretending
The new you is not true you—the real you is ending

Yet, it still doesn't work, and you're left alone
They're at the party while you're stuck at home
But one day you'll find your own people who get you
True friends who will purposefully choose and select you

Daddy

Piggyback rides into the tides
That's where my memories reside
You made me safe—I could not hide
The joy and love I felt inside

Making castles in the sand
Walking while you held my hand
The taste of salt and air and sea
Sunshine beating down on me

Giggling as I looked for shells
Playing catch upon the swells
Of waves that crashed upon the shore
With the father I adored

I always knew that I was loved
Cherished, always placed above
The busyness of life and work
I never doubted I came first

Thank you for the life you lived
You taught me joy and how to give
Time to others—to seize the day
Make moments and memories that will stay

Daddy

I will forever miss your face, your voice, your constant laughter
And though you are no longer here, you taught me that I matter
And every time the sunshine smiles and waves dance on the beach
I'll know the display is just your way to show that you love me

If I Were Claire

Oh, how I wish that I could be Claire—
The girl with the shiny and silky long hair
She floats when she walks, and her voice when she talks
Is joyful and confident—everyone flocks

To be in her presence and be her best friend
I just can't imagine—I can't comprehend
How my life would be better, but I could not ever
Be someone like she is—so gorgeous and clever

If I were Claire, my life would be perfect
I'd never complain, and I'd do all my work, yet
I'd be so smart that I'd get it done fast
I'd impress all the teachers and students in class

I'd be really popular—everyone would be
Obsessed with becoming a best friend with me
I'd never be lonely or feel out of place
I'd walk around school with a smile on my face

Because deep inside I would know I'm the prettiest,
The loveliest, coolest, most talented, wittiest
But I guess I'll forever remain who I am
A simple and plain girl . . . I am just Sam

If I Were Claire

If I Were Sam

Oh, how I wish that I could be Sam
She's capable, strong—have you seen how she can
Run fast like wind, and I cannot begin
To understand how her shots always go in

She doesn't need makeup—she's pretty without it
Her smile is so charming and without any doubt it
Makes everyone comfortable, people respect her
She's kind and she's caring—you never expect her

To get into drama; she doesn't need it
If I could be her, I know I'd succeed at
Being more real—I could be myself
Instead of pretending to be someone else

If I were Sam, my life would be perfect
I'd never complain, and I'd know that my worth is
Not about nails, my clothes, or my hair
Sam is so humble, and yet so aware

I cannot imagine just how it would be
To have all my classmates look up to me
I wish I could be like her—it isn't fair
That I'll forever be stuck as just Claire

Leadership

Everyone tells me that I'm born to lead
But they don't tell me why I'd ever need
To trade in my sanity just for the vanity
Of thinking my power could help out humanity

The political game is filled with the shame
Of telling big lies and then passing the blame
The constant debates are filled with pure hate
No one is listening; people can't wait

To slam others' thoughts even though they cannot
Explain their ideas or connect all the dots
Both sides say they're better—they have the solutions
It seems that they're just tied to large contributions

From those who gain power by spreading more fear
They divide, not unite us, and it is not clear
Why full-grown adults cannot get along
While telling their kids that together we're strong

Please stop igniting all this useless fighting
Your behavior divides us, and it is heightening
The insults you offer instead of suggestions
Instead of real answers, you leave us with questions

And when facts are false or somehow distorted
You add to the drama, and we're not supported
So as I listen and watch as I scroll
Your constant battling's taking its toll

You teach to us—preach to us—to love one another
To support and protect our dear sisters and brothers
Adults now seem cruel, as a general rule
And fixing it's not what we're learning in school

You've left a huge mess for my generation
I hope you will take into consideration
That one can like someone with a different stance
Stop being fake for our sake——give us
a chance

Everyone tells me that I'm born
to lead
But I am not sure that I know
what that means
Step up and do better—you're
the adults
Perhaps if you did, we'd have
better results

The unraveling

I am like thread
Endlessly stitching and mending
Hemming and fixing
Not breaking, but bending

Wound tightly at times
There is no relief
All count on me
In me they believe

I repair and I patch, but
I tangle and knot
Sometimes I grow tired
Yet I know I cannot

My spool snags and spins
It twirls without ceasing
Needles poke me again
Yet still swirling, no releasing

I feel unloosened,
The need to let go
Stretched ever so thin
The unraveling slow

I long for some help
God, please be a tailor
Quilt all the pieces
And save me from failure

Weave me back together
Embroider my heart
Will you make me unbreakable?
Provide a fresh start?

I know I have a purpose
To mend and repair
Stitch into me strength
And peace—that's my prayer

Overscheduled

On Mondays, there's Mandarin from four until six
And then there is swim team because I was picked
For several events to compete in the meet
Eat a late dinner, then I complete
My homework and study for my ACT
Failing is just not an option for me

On Tuesdays, there's chess team and then there's debate
One after the other, so I'm always late
Practice my violin, eat in the car
Drive across town to my lesson—it's far
Read chapter ten riding back home and then
Revise my essay and submit it again

On Wednesdays, I go to my calculus class
Tutoring sessions so I can pass
My classes with A's and not fall behind
Keep grinding and finding there's no extra time
Go practice soccer—my team's in the lead
Work into the night when it's sleep that I need

On Thursdays, I have my piano lessons
Followed by voice class and then acting sessions
I'm not a good singer, but my mom says I can

Become one if I keep practicing and
Besides, I need to be very well rounded
So colleges think that I'm also well grounded

On Fridays there's track team; I don't run too fast
But Mom says it looks good on résumés—they ask
For my activities, my drive, dedication
She wants them to think I'm the best in the nation
So I'll get scholarships; all will accept me
Her dreams live through me; so no one can reject me

On Saturdays I run between games, competitions
It's always the same, and this repetition
Tires me more, despite winning scores
I just want some time so that I can sleep more
I've lost all my friends; there just isn't time
I'm miserable, yet I pretend that I'm fine

Yet Sunday's still not a day I can rest
After church I volunteer and I invest
Time with my family, although it's all forced
The constant pushing me makes me feel worse
Oh, how I wish I could somehow stop time
Or at least find a way to make some of it mine
To wake up and feel the release of this weight
Of goals I don't set but that I'm forced to chase

overscheduled

I Learn Differently

I know that I learn differently
Here is how it works with me:
Sometimes the words don't come on time
They're stuck between my mouth and mind

I have a thought, but expressing it takes
A slower pace, so please wait
I need your patience while I think
To see the links and make them sync

Then I have to read things again
To understand better and comprehend
And when it comes to words to spell
I struggle to do that very well

This can be hard—I get frustrated
Especially when I know I'm graded
I feel embarrassed and want to hide
The challenges I have inside

I know that I learn differently
But I am still capable—watch me and see
I know that in some ways, I'm really smart
I'm good with people, and I shine in art

Numbers click, and I act in plays
It's just the darn words that get stuck on some days
I'm also an athlete who runs really fast
I work very hard, and I pass every class

Please challenge me and expect me to be
A talented student who will still succeed
I go at a speed where some things will take longer
However, I know that this just makes me stronger

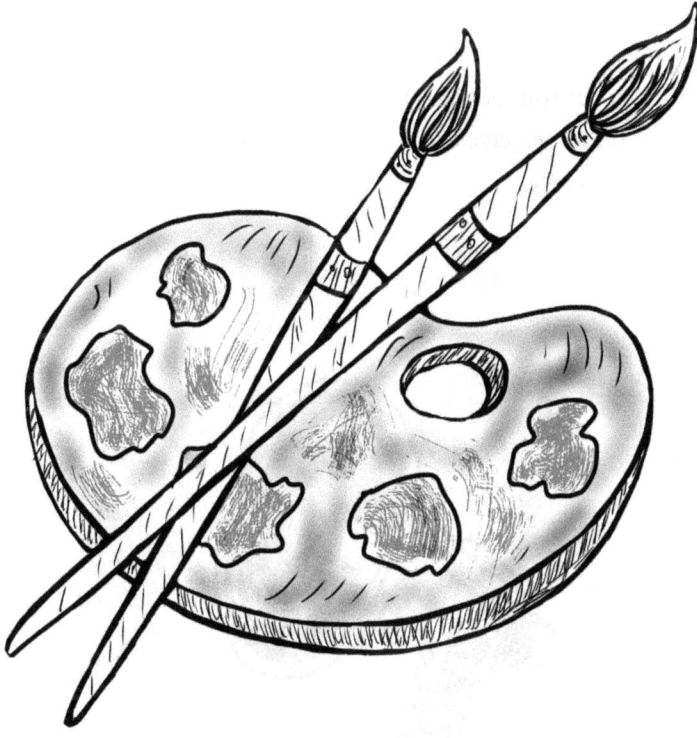

Loud

You always tell me that I am too loud
I'm too much—you hear me above all the crowd
You shush me and hush me and wish I were muted
You give me that look—but I'm not suited
To lower my volume if I am excited
When I feel things deeply, my levels are heightened

Sometimes there's just so much I need to say
The words spill out quickly—my volume's a way
For you to perceive how the things that I shout
Help you receive what I'm talking about

Loud

And on the occasions when I'm being calm
You constantly bug me and ask me what's wrong
You don't like my silence—you don't like my sound
Do you see why I'm not sure I want you around?

I wish you'd accept me—please stop this indictment
Appreciate the ways I express my excitement
Your constant complaining is taking its toll
I won't be adjusted by remote control

Puberty

I know you told me I soon would be changing
But you did not mention this whole rearranging
Of my body parts and how they would start
Growing so fast 'cause my hormones are raging

You told me I might find that there is more hair
But jeez, you didn't explain it'd be there!
And despite all my trying, I cannot stop crying
One minute I'm joyful, the next in despair

You mentioned it all like this thing would be simple,
But each passing hour there's a festering red pimple
That grows on this face that's completely replaced
The one I was born with—the cute one with dimples

And what is the deal with this underarm smell
I've showered again and I've washed myself well
My clothes are too tight; they don't fit me despite
I am healthy—it's like every part of me swelled

I'll spare you the details of the other stuff
But c'mon—these changes can be very tough
Can I send it back? Is there a way I can drop it?
I hate this puberty. Seriously, please stop it

Puberty

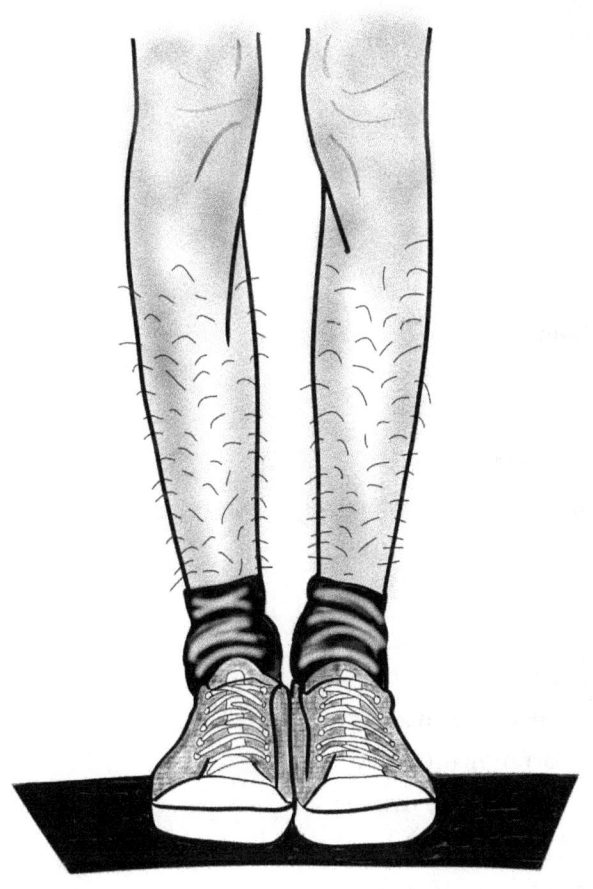

A Good Day

Today was a good day
A nothing in my way day
A say what I mean day
No one was mean day

I woke up on time day
My hair—it felt fine day
My homework was less day
A there was no test day

A pizza to eat day
A warm chocolate treat day
A new friend to meet day
A good front row seat day

A teacher who cared day
She made us prepared day
Felt smart in math day
Was picked for the cast day

A time with my mom day
Laughter and some fun day
My dad came back home day
I was not alone day

A Good Day

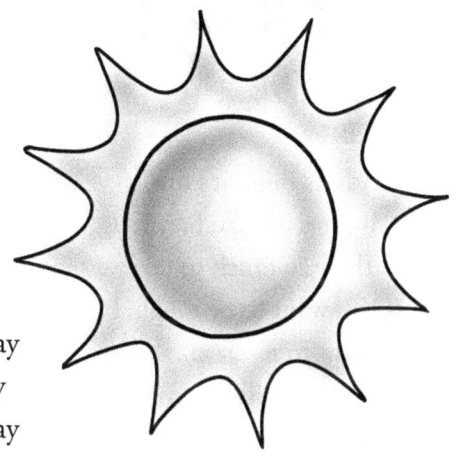

Sat round the table day
Long as I was able day
Had yummy dinner day
Felt like a winner day

A chores were done fast day
A quick game of catch day
Beautiful, clear weather day
Movie all together day

A nice soothing shower day
Relaxed for an hour day
Crawled into bed day
Thankful prayers said day

Dog at my feet day
Eyelids growing weak day
Time to get good rest day
For today was the best day

It's Hard to Be Young
for Clark

Adults think it's fun
But it's hard to be young
There so much to do and required of you
You want to be tough, but are you enough?
Want to reach manhood—do what a young man should
But you still haven't yet finished your childhood
So you struggle, flex muscle to get some respect
Only to find that some still will reject
The person you show them—you're afraid they'll neglect
To understand you and what you want next
So you swallow your sorrow and then bite your tongue
Adults think it's easy
But it's hard to be young

It's hard to be young
When you are among
Others who also are struggling with some
Of the challenges of growing up—finding a voice
Can't measure the pressure to make the right choice
You want independence, be on your own
Must be respectful and use the right tone
But all around you are boys with
Their games and their toys if
They sway you and play you
They become your decoys and

It's Hard to Be Young

You should stay on task, but you wear the mask
Of someone who knows all—you don't want to ask
Sometimes it just seems you're the only one
Who feels deep inside that
It's hard to be young

It's hard to be young
At a school that is fun
Where it's always your job to get your work done
You have to be still when it's all skill and drill
Even the drum cannot subdue the thrill
Of a little mischief—it's all good until
You get that detention . . . you're fearful and still
You find yourself tempted again and again
Although you know you just want to make friends
You want to be cool but still do well in school
Make others laugh, but still follow the rules
And although you're surrounded by cheers, celebrations
Everyone watches with high expectations
You want to be picked to play in the game
You want to make shots—have fans scream your name

Although it's a grand place, there are goals to attain
A legacy to leave when you no longer remain
So others realize that you are someone
That might sound simple
But it's hard to be young

It's hard to be young
When you are someone's son
With great parents who love you—you are their one
Their pride, their joy—no heir to compare to
The hope that they have for the life you've begun
You need to do well
So they know—they can tell that
You are grateful and thankful
When each day is done
Can't catch an attitude—never complain
Even when body or heart feels in pain
You want to be everything—show no defiance
Even when angry, you must be compliant
Do not disappoint them—you must be your best
Do all your chores and pass every test
And although their deep love is second to none
Sometimes with parents
It's hard to be young

It's hard to be young
When you know there's someone
Who believes in you—sees you—
The good you have done
She knows that there's kindness and brilliance inside
Under the silliness and puffed-up false pride
A teacher who notices when there's a smile
Making her day and others' worthwhile
She will still fuss and tell you to stop
She knows if she doesn't, then you might not

It's Hard to Be Young

Embrace all your talents and use all your gifts
As you grow older, she knows you will shift
You'll realize your purpose; you'll know your worth
You will make changes—a difference on earth
Yes, she is old, but her time is not done
Because she remembers that
It's hard to be young

Discussion Questions

There are a variety of ways that one can use these poems to elicit meaningful reflection and discussion. Whether you are discussing one specific poem or several poems at once, the following questions can help drive the conversation.

1. What message or lesson is the person in the poem trying to communicate? How can this message help us better understand others' perspectives?
2. What specific challenges or pressures does the person in the poem face, and how can adults provide better support in situations like this?
3. How does the person in the poem express the need for empathy, attention, or understanding? What can we learn from this?
4. How does the theme of resilience appear in the poem? What strengths does the person show, and how can we foster resilience in young people in a healthy way?
5. What role(s) do the actions play in the poem, and how do these actions impact the relationships and outcomes?
6. How did the person in the poem help you understand how they feel? Have you ever felt the same way? What steps can we take to make young people feel more included and valued?

7. What role does communication—both verbal and nonverbal—play in the poem? How can we improve the way we communicate with young people to show understanding and support?
8. What insights can the poem offer about the balance between independence and support in a young person's life? How can adults guide without hovering or controlling?
9. Did the poem provide insight into how young people are sometimes misjudged by others? How can we teach others not to judge someone else's situation?
10. After reading the poem, were you prompted to think about a situation or a young person in a way you had not considered before? If so, how?

About Kim Bearden

Kim Bearden is the cofounder, executive director, and language arts teacher at the highly acclaimed Ron Clark Academy. Over 150,000 educators from around the world have visited her classroom and attended her workshops to discover innovative ways to engage students, promote academic excellence, build relationships, foster creativity, and cultivate a dynamic school culture.

Throughout her career, Kim has received numerous accolades. She was inducted into the National Teachers Hall of Fame and honored at the White House for her contributions to education. Chosen from over 70,000 nominations, she was named the Disney American Teacher Awards Outstanding Humanities Teacher, and she received the Milken Family Foundation's Award for Excellence in Education. Her other honors include the InfluencHer Award, the University of Georgia Outstanding Educator Award, and the Turknett Character Award for Servant Leadership. She was also featured in Mercedes-Benz's *Greatness Lives Here* campaign and recognized by Women Works Media Group as one of Georgia's Most Powerful and Influential Women.

With a career spanning 39 years, Kim has served as a teacher, instructional lead teacher, curriculum director, school-board member, staff-development trainer, and middle school principal. As both an educator and a mother, she has spent decades listening to, learning from, and supporting children, an experience that gave her unique insight into their thoughts, struggles, and emotions—insight that has shaped her poetry. She is also the bestselling author of four other books: *Fight Song, Talk to Me, Crash Course,* and *The House Where We Belong.*

Kim lives near Atlanta with her husband, Scotty, and is a proud mother of four adult children, all of whom reside in the metro Atlanta area. This book is especially meaningful to her, as it marks a special collaboration with her daughter, Madison, who illustrated the poetry with a depth of artistry and insight that brings each piece to life.

About Madison Hunt

Madison Hunt has been creating art since she could hold a crayon, and her passion for all things artistic—sketching, painting, and beyond—has only grown with time. As the illustrator of *I Really Need You to Hear This*, Madison brought her creative vision to life, choosing to represent many of the poems symbolically while providing insightful contributions to her mother's writing. This book marks her first official role as an illustrator, a collaboration that blends her artistic talent with her deep connection to the words on the page.

Beyond illustration, Madison is a hair artist and the proud owner of MadLove Hair Studio, where she continues to express her creativity through styling. She is a phenomenal daughter, sister, and wife to her eighth-grade sweetheart, Taylor. During the creation of this book, she embarked on another exciting journey—learning that she is expecting her first child.

Madison's artistry, both in life and on paper, makes this book all the more special, reflecting her heart, talent, and love for storytelling through images.

More from Dave Burgess Consulting, Inc.

Since 2012, DBCI has published books that inspire and equip educators to be their best. For more information on our titles or to purchase bulk orders for your school, district, or book study, visit DaveBurgessConsulting.com/DBCIbooks.

The *Like a PIRATE*™ Series

Teach Like a PIRATE by Dave Burgess
eXPlore Like a PIRATE by Michael Matera
Learn Like a PIRATE by Paul Solarz
Plan Like a PIRATE by Dawn M. Harris
Play Like a PIRATE by Quinn Rollins
Run Like a PIRATE by Adam Welcome
Tech Like a PIRATE by Matt Miller

The *Lead Like a PIRATE*™ Series

Lead Like a PIRATE by Shelley Burgess and Beth Houf
Balance Like a PIRATE by Jessica Cabeen, Jessica Johnson, and Sarah Johnson
Lead beyond Your Title by Nili Bartley
Lead with Appreciation by Amber Teamann and Melinda Miller
Lead with Collaboration by Allyson Apsey and Jessica Gomez
Lead with Culture by Jay Billy
Lead with Instructional Rounds by Vicki Wilson
Lead with Literacy by Mandy Ellis
She Leads by Dr. Rachael George and Majalise W. Tolan

The *EduProtocol Field Guide* Series

Deploying EduProtocols by Kim Voge, with Jon Corippo and Marlena Hebern

The EduProtocol Field Guide by Marlena Hebern and Jon Corippo

The EduProtocol Field Guide Book 2 by Marlena Hebern and Jon Corippo

The EduProtocol Field Guide Math Edition by Lisa Nowakowski and Jeremiah Ruesch

The EduProtocol Field Guide Primary Edition by Benjamin Cogswell and Jennifer Dean

The EduProtocol Field Guide Social Studies Edition by Dr. Scott M. Petri and Adam Moler

The EduProtocol Field Guide ELA Edition by Jacob Carr

Leadership & School Culture

Be 1% Better by Ron Clark

Be THAT Teacher by Dwayne Reed

Beyond the Surface of Restorative Practices by Marisol Rerucha

Change the Narrative by Henry J. Turner and Kathy Lopes

Choosing to See by Pamela Seda and Kyndall Brown

Culturize by Jimmy Casas

Discipline Win by Andy Jacks

Educate Me! by Dr. Shree Walker with Micheal D. Ison

Escaping the School Leader's Dunk Tank by Rebecca Coda and Rick Jetter

Fight Song by Kim Bearden

From Teacher to Leader by Starr Sackstein

If the Dance Floor Is Empty, Change the Song by Joe Clark

The Innovator's Mindset by George Couros

It's OK to Say "They" by Christy Whittlesey

Kids Deserve It! by Todd Nesloney and Adam Welcome

Leading the Whole Teacher by Allyson Apsey

Let Them Speak by Rebecca Coda and Rick Jetter
The Limitless School by Abe Hege and Adam Dovico
Live Your Excellence by Jimmy Casas
Next-Level Teaching by Jonathan Alsheimer
The Pepper Effect by Sean Gaillard
Principaled by Kate Barker, Kourtney Ferrua, and Rachael George
The Principled Principal by Jeffrey Zoul and Anthony McConnell
Relentless by Hamish Brewer
The Secret Solution by Todd Whitaker, Sam Miller, and Ryan Donlan
Start. Right. Now. by Todd Whitaker, Jeffrey Zoul, and Jimmy Casas
Stop. Right. Now. by Jimmy Casas and Jeffrey Zoul
Teach Your Class Off by CJ Reynolds
Teachers Deserve It by Rae Hughart and Adam Welcome
They Call Me "Mr. De" by Frank DeAngelis
Thrive through the Five by Jill M. Siler
Unmapped Potential by Julie Hasson and Missy Lennard
When Kids Lead by Todd Nesloney and Adam Dovico
Word Shift by Joy Kirr
Your School Rocks by Ryan McLane and Eric Lowe

Technology & Tools

50 Things to Go Further with Google Classroom by Alice Keeler and Libbi Miller
50 Things You Can Do with Google Classroom by Alice Keeler and Libbi Miller
50 Ways to Engage Students with Google Apps by Alice Keeler and Heather Lyon
140 Twitter Tips for Educators by Brad Currie, Billy Krakower, and Scott Rocco

Block Breaker by Brian Aspinall

Building Blocks for Tiny Techies by Jamila "Mia" Leonard

Code Breaker by Brian Aspinall

The Complete EdTech Coach by Katherine Goyette and Adam Juarez

Control Alt Achieve by Eric Curts

The Esports Education Playbook by Chris Aviles, Steve Isaacs, Christine Lion-Bailey, and Jesse Lubinsky

Google Apps for Littles by Christine Pinto and Alice Keeler

Master the Media by Julie Smith

Raising Digital Leaders by Jennifer Casa-Todd

Reality Bytes by Christine Lion-Bailey, Jesse Lubinsky, and Micah Shippee, PhD

Sail the 7 Cs with Microsoft Education by Becky Keene and Kathi Kersznowski

Shake Up Learning by Kasey Bell

Social LEADia by Jennifer Casa-Todd

Stepping Up to Google Classroom by Alice Keeler and Kimberly Mattina

Teaching Math with Google Apps by Alice Keeler and Diana Herrington

Teaching with Google Jamboard by Alice Keeler and Kimberly Mattina

Teachingland by Amanda Fox and Mary Ellen Weeks

Teaching Methods & Materials

All 4s and 5s by Andrew Sharos

Boredom Busters by Katie Powell

Building Strong Writers by Christina Schneider

The Classroom Chef by John Stevens and Matt Vaudrey

The Collaborative Classroom by Trevor Muir

Copyrighteous by Diana Gill

More from Dave Burgess Consulting, Inc.

CREATE by Bethany J. Petty
Ditch That Homework by Matt Miller and Alice Keeler
Ditch That Textbook by Matt Miller
Don't Ditch That Tech by Matt Miller, Nate Ridgway, and Angelia Ridgway
EDrenaline Rush by John Meehan
Educated by Design by Michael Cohen, The Tech Rabbi
Empowered to Choose: A Practical Guide to Personalized Learning by Andrew Easton
Expedition Science by Becky Schnekser
Frustration Busters by Katie Powell
Fully Engaged by Michael Matera and John Meehan
Game On? Brain On! by Lindsay Portnoy, PhD
Guided Math AMPED by Reagan Tunstall
Happy & Resilient by Roni Habib
Innovating Play by Jessica LaBar-Twomy and Christine Pinto
Instant Relevance by Denis Sheeran
Instructional Coaching Connection by Nathan Lang-Raad
Keeping the Wonder by Jenna Copper, Ashley Bible, Abby Gross, and Staci Lamb
LAUNCH by John Spencer and A.J. Juliani
Learning in the Zone by Dr. Sonny Magana
Lights, Cameras, TEACH! by Kevin J. Butler
Make Learning MAGICAL by Tisha Richmond
Pass the Baton by Kathryn Finch and Theresa Hoover
Project-Based Learning Anywhere by Lori Elliott
Pure Genius by Don Wettrick
The Revolution by Darren Ellwein and Derek McCoy
The Science Box by Kim Adsit and Adam Peterson
Shift This! by Joy Kirr
Skyrocket Your Teacher Coaching by Michael Cary Sonbert
Spark Learning by Ramsey Musallam

Sparks in the Dark by Travis Crowder and Todd Nesloney
Table Talk Math by John Stevens
Teachables by Cheryl Abla and Lisa Maxfield
Unpack Your Impact by Naomi O'Brien and LaNesha Tabb
The Wild Card by Hope and Wade King
Writefully Empowered by Jacob Chastain
The Writing on the Classroom Wall by Steve Wyborney
You Are Poetry by Mike Johnston
You'll Never Guess What I'm Saying by Naomi O'Brien
You'll Never Guess What I'm Thinking About by Naomi O'Brien

Inspiration, Professional Growth & Personal Development

Be REAL by Tara Martin
Be the One for Kids by Ryan Sheehy
The Coach ADVenture by Amy Illingworth
Creatively Productive by Lisa Johnson
The Ed Branding Book by Dr. Renae Bryant and Lynette White
Educational Eye Exam by Alicia Ray
The EduNinja Mindset by Jennifer Burdis
Empower Our Girls by Lynmara Colón and Adam Welcome
Finding Lifelines by Andrew Grieve and Andrew Sharos
The Four O'Clock Faculty by Rich Czyz
How Much Water Do We Have? by Pete and Kris Nunweiler
P Is for Pirate by Dave and Shelley Burgess
A Passion for Kindness by Tamara Letter
The Path to Serendipity by Allyson Apsey
PheMOMenal Teacher by Annick Rauch
Recipes for Resilience by Robert A. Martinez
Rogue Leader by Rich Czyz
Sanctuaries by Dan Tricarico
Saving Sycamore by Molly B. Hudgens

The Secret Sauce by Rich Czyz
Shattering the Perfect Teacher Myth by Aaron Hogan
Stories from Webb by Todd Nesloney
Talk to Me by Kim Bearden
Teach Better by Chad Ostrowski, Tiffany Ott, Rae Hughart, and Jeff Gargas
Teach Me, Teacher by Jacob Chastain
Teach, Play, Learn! by Adam Peterson
Teaching Is a Tattoo by Mike Johnston
The Teachers of Oz by Herbie Raad and Nathan Lang-Raad
Teaching the Ms. Abbott Way by Joyce Stephens Abbott
TeamMakers by Laura Robb and Evan Robb
Through the Lens of Serendipity by Allyson Apsey
Write Here and Now by Dan Tricarico
The Zen Teacher by Dan Tricarico

Children's Books

The Adventures of Little Mickey by Mickey Smith Jr.
Alpert by LaNesha Tabb
Alpert & Friends by LaNesha Tabb
Beyond Us by Aaron Polansky
Cannonball In by Tara Martin
Dolphins in Trees by Aaron Polansky
Dragon Smart by Tisha and Tommy Richmond
I Can Achieve Anything by MoNique Waters
I Want to Be a Lot by Ashley Savage
The Magic of Wonder by Jenna Copper, Ashley Bible, Abby Gross, and Staci Lamb
Micah's Big Question by Naomi O'Brien
The Princes of Serendip by Allyson Apsey
Ride with Emilio by Richard Nares
A Teacher's Top Secret Confidential by LaNesha Tabb

A Teacher's Top Secret: Mission Accomplished by LaNesha Tabb
The Wild Card Kids by Hope and Wade King
Zom-Be a Design Thinker by Amanda Fox

www.ingramcontent.com/pod-product-compliance
Lightning Source LLC
Chambersburg PA
CBHW050554160426
43199CB00015B/2657